CW00376056

PERHAPS GOD. . .

Also by the Author:
Life Is Simpler Towards Evening
Ripples of Stillness

PERHAPS GOD. . .

by

RALPH WRIGHT, O.S.B.

THE GOLDEN QUILL PRESS
Publishers
Francestown   New Hampshire

© RALPH WRIGHT 1985

Library of Congress Catalog Card Number 85-81668

ISBN 0-8233-0411-6

Printed in the United States of America

ACKNOWLEDGEMENTS

I would like to acknowledge with gratitude the following magazines in which some of these poems originally appeared. In the United States: *America, New Oxford Review, University of Portland Review*; in the United Kingdom: *The Tablet*. I would also like to thank the Daughters of Saint Paul for permission to include the poems "Donkey" and "Ground for Joy" which first appeared in a collection of my poems that they published entitled *Ripples of Stillness*.

"...that my own joy may be in you
and your joy be complete."

John 15.11

"You spoke just now as though he had been
cured." "I really think he was. He'd learned
to serve other people, you see, and to laugh.
An odd laugh, but it was a laugh all the same.
I'm frightened of people who don't laugh."

A Burnt-Out Case (p. 247)
Graham Greene

CONTENTS

Limericks

PERHAPS GOD. . .

PERHAPS GOD

perhaps God
who cannot logically
know surprise
became Man
who can
so that his Pneuma
might share Man's humor
so maybe a part
of the explanation
for the Incarnation
- or even half -
was to give God
a good laugh

CANA

there was far
too much wine
at Cana
for there to be no laughter

and Jesus added to it

WHEN GOD MADE YOU

When
God
made
you
there
was
silence
in
heaven
for
five
minutes.
Then
God
said:
"How come I never thought of that before?"

POEM

a poem is an acrid
semi-ecstatic
immaterial
sneeze
breaking beautifully
out of silence
after a moment's
pause
poised
outside history
taking flesh in scrawl and revealing
the mind's mystery

FOOL

Fool—I said to myself—
why so proud of being
for such a brief
flash in the wide
pan of the universe
somebody—master of all—
standing and fronting the sun
but unable to be
for more than the sigh that it takes
to grow old—
Fool—I said—be your age
be intensely
be molten and rage
be loud be colored be new
be open be air
be there
to breathe and be breathed
but be not deceived
be awake be aware
of your size and be proud
—if at all—
Fool be proud
be proud
to be small

DRAGONFLIES

dragonflies
mate in mid-air
and have done it this way
for a hundred million years

if it's poor
helicoptrics
to mate while revolving
they're mighty slow
getting the message
and evolving

HAIKU?

God laughing
me into being
and you too -
a joke to remember.

CATERPILLAR
thoughts on weeding

the caterpillar
  chews and chews
deliberately
  on greens and blues

does he with joy
  accept his fate
a munching, crawling,
  stalk-bound state

or does he in
  the dark of night
dream of the ecstasy
  of flight

till from his tomb
  like Egypt's kings
he soars on silent
  cosmic wings

and nectar unconceived
  before
sips from a brief
  ambrosial straw?

HYGIENE

The janitor of our world, God,
Man tells him, doesn't know his job.
The oceans, rivers, lakes and streams
are thick with life that spawns and teems.
So God is fired and Man assumes
his role with mops and swabs and brooms.
He purges all the planet's waste
with acids poured with human grace.
With oil he sweeps the ocean floor
of seaweed, shark and man-of-war.
And when at last the planet's clean
those jungle days are just a dream.
The ache of life has left his head;
he is awake and clean and dead.

FUZZY TECHNOCRATS

The fuzzy caterpillars know
this year there won't be too much snow.
By going minkless they declare
that winter will be less severe.

The graduated weather men
predict the cold extreme again.
The spots upon the sun proclaim
the truth, they say, of what they claim.

So spoke October, now at ease
we watch as January recedes
and snowless we observe a fact
that should perhaps have some impact:

in this our technocratic age
when swift computers are the rage
the Doctors who had scanned the sun
were wrong when all is said and done.

The caterpillars had foretold
a winter neither long nor cold.
Wise nature with no high degrees
spoke quietly and there was no freeze.

MR. SKUNK R.I.P.

Liquidated
in the wee hours
by a drunk driver

you left your comment
on the landscape
for miles around

that we might get the message
'All Flesh Is Gas'
and mourn your passing.

BEFUDDLED

A slow befuddled winter fly
  with 747 abandon
has trundled from my window sill
  and God knows what he'll land on.

Such geriatric flies present
  a crisis to compassion:
to smear them or to leave them space
  to die in their own fashion.

RAISON D'ETRE SOPHOMORE

thoughts on supervising sophomore
end of year exam 1974

God's inscrutable infinite mind
  seeking eternally something to do
of all the possible human kind
  ended up creating you.

His ways are wonderful and mysterious
  so don't ask me why
'cos all I'd say if you put it to me
  is "Well done, God, nice try!"

MEDITATION AT SUNDAY LITURGY

God loves me, yet
  I still abuse
myself, my neighbor
  and these pews.

God loves me, yet
  I try to please
the World in ones
  and twos and threes.

God loves me, yet
  I still abhor
the drunk, the lecher
  and the bore.

God loves me, why
  am I not free
to be as God
  would have me be?

TRANSPLANT

The surgeon—Master of the arts—
has learnt to plant organic parts
but never will and never can
effect a change of heart in Man
for God alone
has the craft
in place of human hearts of stone
to graft his own.

PROBLEM OF EVIL

God made Man free
  to get things wrong:
He made the atom,
  we the bomb.

ROBOT CRIB

A robot shepherd
a robot star
a robot child
on real straw
sucking real milk
from a robot maid
with a robot king
in gold braid
bringing real myrrh
to the really conscious
cybernetic
divine babe
(man made)
who then says
in a couple of whirs
with a wide grin
that he prefers
real men
and real sin
—you can't win!

I KNOW A MAN WHO HAS A FEEL
FOR LEAVES

I know a man who has a feel for leaves
and treats them kindly as one might a friend
he feels that if a human being were cloned
and multiplied like paper-backs or waves
they still would have a being of their own
and would when gone be left in separate graves

so why not have a reverence for each leaf
like this one from an oak tree on this path
reaching like a hand towards who knows
what dying ecstasy as the slow breeze
helps it find a resting place or home
in the recycling earth?

He feels that it is worth
a moment's silence and believes
that anyone who ever has seen war
or heard of famines, floods or on the news
has watched the havoc that an earthquake
        strewed
with men and mountains in its wake ignored
—or even watched a stadiumful applaud—
will pause with wonder as he lookes and
        breathes
and also have a little time for leaves.

GOD'S CHANCE OF MUSIC

Time is God's vast
sense of humor
a rampant melodious
half-mysterious
semi-courteous
practical joke
on men microbes
rocks rhinos
thinkers and things
flung in an ordered
pattern of tight con-
tinuous moments
into being
a long queue
for Fish & Chips
waiting in line to be different.

Can you see
the vast joke
of suddenly being
and never the same?
Isn't this
an absurd game
for an Almighty
to want to play?
Yet if our reasoning minds refuse it
time still remains
—a clown might say—
God's chance of music.

31

DONKEY

my ears are long
and though I'm small
I remain
unworried

I'm rather slow
when urged to go
and like to be
unhurried

when men see me
they tend to smile
and this is good
'cos for a while

I bore in triumph
through the streets
the God of joy
and Man of peace
—a dignity
that keeps

NO TWO SNOWFLAKES

no two snowflakes
have the same
size weight
or even shape
every leaf
is unique
every person's
brand of hair
grows in fact
no other where
dust the world
then blow and find
infinite prints
left behind
from God's own fingers
like a word
spoken on a
frosty day
that in the silence
lingers

LIFE

Life is like Leonardo on a pavement
chalking Mona Lisa
he caught the moment but the rain came
taking her person and her smile away
when it stopped he took his empty cap
and went home laughing.

TWO FOOLS

two tumble in space
but only one
knows the comedy
of being wrong

one fool
with a foot on the moon
forgets the hands
at the Potter's wheel

one knows
the Clown Creator
shaping clay
into laughter

two tumble in space
but only one
knows that tragedy
will be gone

TICK-TOCK

The space between
the tick and the tock
is a million years
in the Father's clock.
Think of this
when the days seem long.
The stars are right.
Your watch is wrong.

PLATITUDE—a definition

a platitude
is an overchewed
fact
that lacks
everything that might
afford delight

APATHY 10,000,000

This line of noughts tells the years
that science counts since we began
how odd that after such travail
the earth should yawn and I should come
but dumb-confounding that I know
the jaws will close and back I'll go
yet think it is of small avail
whether in this brief hour I fail
to love or hate win or lose
seek or find receive or choose
and while I frown smile and live
as dull and mediocre clay
can humankind or God forgive
a life so monotoned in gray
subrational unconcerned and slack
I take my bow and won't be back.

EACH SINGLE GRAIN

Pressed
navel down
against
the warm white powder
while the sun
bronzes my body dry
I find gravel
against my teeth
and think of computers
calculating
in the blink of an eye
each single grain
drying
upon my body
upon this beach
on all the beaches of the planet
and I think of Abraham
lying upon it
navel to the desert sky
watching by night
the milkwash of the galaxies
and dreaming of Isaac I hear him say
'No way!'

ODE TO A GRECIAN BLARNEYMAN

he speaks as casually
as normal people breathe
unaware totally
of the worth of words
while all the while his eyes
always without guile
speak of what it means to be alive
and wild
upon the brief adventure of this planet
shot by God like a bottle rocket
on the 4th
into the dark night sky

SOBER THOUGHT

Father, if you love me
as much as you love your Son
I'd better watch out.
Look what they did to Him!

being older
is being conscious
of being bones

posing the question
as right and proper
of the dust doorway
with the skull knocker

daring to plunge
in thoughts of void
or kingdom come

being older
is tasting life
with a new tongue
knowing the sap
will fail to run

seeing new
touching new
loving new

and being bolder
for being bones

GROUND FOR JOY

My past lies
in the merciful hands of God
my future
in his wise love
the present moment
in which I live
is of no duration
how then may fear win
mastery over my joy?

REFLECTIONS re PRODUCTION

God gave sex joy to help mankind
  beget and be begotten.
He gave kids charm that they might be
  beloved and not forgotten.
He made the teenage youth
  arrogant and uncouth
that being a kind of pain in the nest
  quite soon he'd be given the hoof.
And though this remains upsetting
  it's God's way to get him begetting.

Limericks

KENTUCKY

A horse-breeding monk from Kentucky,
His habit all rent and all mucky,
    Used to nail horses' shoes
    To his brethren's pews
'Cos he said that their prayers was unlucky.

UTAH

An old scottish Abbot in Utah
believes that all Tomcats are newtah
He makes a wee pittance
producing grey kittens
in test-tubes entirely of pewtah.

PERU

A wine-drinking monk from Peru,
whose thoughts are remarkably few,
    thinks the drinking of wine
    makes one's thinking sublime
which he thought when he'd had one or two.

HAVANA

A bomb-building monk from Havana,
Who had an unfortunate stammer,
    Gave a cry 'b.b.bomb!'
    He was late but not wrong
And his relics descended like manna.

VANCOUVER

A little old nun from Vancouver
By a smooth cadillac was run ouver.
    There was no bump,
    The driver was drunk,
So nobody came to remove her.

WISCONSIN

A dissolute monk from Wisconsin
Discovered the world's greatest non-sin.
    With the purest intention
    He sold the invention
And squandered the takings upon sin.

ELMIRA

A frantic young friar from Elmira
Preached threats that got direr and direr,
    Till the congregation
    Accepted damnation
And changed the town's name to 'Elfire-a.

YALE

An abbot who majored at Yale
Got involved in a scandalous tale.
　　He took to grass
　　And ended, alas,
Demoted, defrocked and in jail.

FLORIDA

There was a young hermit from Florida
Whose nightmares got horrider and horrider.
    Till the piercing screams
    Of these terrible dreams
Made his neighbors get worrida and worrida.

MANILA

A hermit who prays near Manila
Used to hit with a lady guerrilla
    Till his temper got frayed
    And he served a grenade
In a futile endeavor to kill her.

UKRAINE

A patriarch from the Ukraine,
Whose tennis is largely in vain,
    Swings wide at the ball,
    Never hits it at all
And everyone else is to blame.

XANADU-ROME

Pope Kubla from Xanadu-Rome
Built a Vatican Sports Pleasure-Dome,
    Whence he served to far places
    Encyclical aces
On balls branded 'Ex-Cathedrome'.

PEKING

A bishop who hits in Peking
Can serve with incredible spin.
    His favorite slice
    Goes around the court twice
And the third time around it falls in.

IRAN

A smooth young recluse from Iran,
Who oozes a cadillac charm,
    Is perfecting his aces
    In private oases
With rackets entirely of palm.

FRANCE

A drop-shooting sister from France,
Whose feet tread a lyrical dance,
    Should give some reflection
    To more genuflection
For grace should leave nothing to Chance.

HONOLULU

A guru who combs Honolulu
Has a grip that's as rigid as glue-lu.
  Though his backswing is smooth
  As fingers that soothe
Alas, he has no follow-through-lu.

JAPAN

A young Buddhist monk from Japan,
Who ponders the essence of Man,
    With a noble reserve
    Can return any serve
And he knows with calm that he can.

YOKOHAMA

An abbess from fair Yokohama
Plays tennis with God without drama.
    Though He serves from above
    And the score's forty—love
Yet nothing He does can alarm her.

CRETE

A compassionate Abbess from Crete
Found it desperately hard to compete.
    When winning a game
    She would feel so much shame
That she'd pray for the grace of defeat.

LEEDS

When a highly-strung bishop from Leeds,
Whose ulcer still pains him and bleeds,
    Diverts his high tensions
    To cat-gut dimensions
His thoughts are as calm as his deeds.

SOAP TRAGEDY

it didn't seem
somehow right
to kill the General
with a kitchen knife

so she quietly seized
a Greek axe
and felled her hubby
with three hacks

thus Clytemnestra
with a ghastly laugh
killed Agamemnon
in the bath